Children Have Basic Rights

Elliot Paderewski

Rosen REAL READERS

Rosen Classroom™
New York

My name is Brett.

I am on my way to school.

This is my teacher, Ms. Green. She is teaching us about children's rights.

Ms. Green says that children have many rights.
We have the right to learn.
We go to school to learn.

We have the right to safety. A crossing guard helps us get to school.

Children have the right to
be safe at school.
We feel safe in our classrooms.

Children have the right to be heard.

Our teachers want to hear what we have to say.

Children have the right to food.
We eat lunch together.
Ms. Green makes sure
everyone has food.

Ms. Green says that children have rights outside of school. Children have the right to a place to live.

We also have a right to health care.

This means that children can see a doctor if they are sick.

Children who work have rights. They cannot work long hours at a job.

Words to Know

children

classroom

crossing guard

doctor

food

teacher